DEATH, LIFE & DISCIPLESHIP

Seven Ways Jesus Defeated Death Before the Resurrection

Victor Collins

Printed in the United States of America
First Printing, 2024
ISBN 978-1-954658-15-8

Pre-submission editor - Heidi Titus

The Well Publishers
PMB #533
520 Butternut Dr., Suite 8
Holland, MI 49424
https://thewellpublishers.com

Endorsements for Death, Life & Discipleship

"Here is a wonderful walk through the issue of life and death from a biblical perspective. The story of life first given in Eden by our Loving Creator, of life threatened by both temporal and eternal death through the scourge of sin, and the new and eternal life announced in the gospel and made available through Jesus Christ... this story gives shape and sense to the whole Christian journey...now and into eternity. Collins reliably and helpfully leads his readers into and through the contours of this macro-story."

Joseph Dongell – Professor of Biblical Studies, Asbury Theological Seminary

"My friend, Victor Collins has done an excellent job of presenting a fresh perspective on the gospel of Mark. By highlighting seven ways Jesus defeated death BEFORE his own resurrection, he challenges us to discover the life-giving, sin-defeating, storm-calming, demon-chasing power of Christian discipleship. By alerting us to the fact that "death comes to humans in many forms," Vic points us to spiritual resources that God has given us in the gospel to enable us to "choose life" (Deut. 30:19). It is a joy to recommend this book."

Stan Key – OneWay Ministries

"In this clearly-written book the author shows how the making of disciples is God's means of restoring life to a world in which death has become dominant. In each chapter he takes a Biblical incident or incident and shows how God confronts and conquers death in the experience(s) of those persons. Each chapter closes with a list of principles learned and questions for discussion. The book's clarity and brevity will make it attractive to lay groups looking for study materials."

Dr. John Oswalt – Book of Isaiah, New International Commentary on the Old Testament (NICOT)

"So clear, so pastoral, biblical, relevant … Many need to read this … Engaging and deep without being condescending … I love your focus on accountability and disciple-making throughout."

Dr. Bill Ury – National Ambassador of Holiness, Salvation Army

Table of Contents

Dedication

To Sue, my wife, and my friend.
"We are writing these things so that
our joy may be complete." (1 John 1:4)

Death, Life & Discipleship

The Last Enemy (Introduction)

Looking at the amazing life spans of the first generations of human beings, we see some astronomical numbers in terms of years lived. The longevity of Adam, Seth, Kenan, and Methuselah staggers the imagination![1] The life spans they enjoyed are certainly not the life spans we experience. However, there is a short phrase used by the author of Genesis depicting their reality that we still use today: "And he died."[2] We often skim right

---

[1] See the Book of Genesis Chapter 5 in any Holy Bible.
[2] Ibid. Consistently the last three words in the story of each person's life.

past that statement and marvel at the number of years our forerunners lived. God wants those three simple words to move us deeply. Death, the first enemy on the scene and the last enemy to be defeated, takes a heavy toll on humanity.

We miss the fact that, according to Genesis 1-2, God intended life to be our forever condition. In response to our discovery that Methuselah had a limit to the years he lived, our eyes should well up with tears. We should be anguished reading that his life was cut short. His 969 years were but a brief nano-moment in terms of the eternity that he could have had. We were meant to live forever. Sin, ushering in death, had to be dealt with.

The very nature of God is life-giving, life-multiplying. He did not just create a few fish and hope they would proliferate. God reveals, *"the waters swarmed after their kind"* (Genesis 1:21). God created life in abundance! Death was not a part of the picture. Yet, from Genesis 3 up to the present day we too repeat the phrase, "and he died" to reflect the reality of all those who have gone before us. This phrase is repeated ad nauseum in Genesis 5. God is trying to get our attention. He is going to provide a way to overthrow death, along with grief and despair.

He is the God of life, not death. We can hear His voice echo from ages past, "This is not of Me. As people of a Living God, we too should reject being resigned to it. It was never to be this way!" Still, our eyes return to the amazing number of life years, and we wonder what it must have been like. God's heart aches for us to live and experience true life. We can feel it in His call to life, *"I have set before you life and death … choose life in order that you may live"* (Deuteronomy 30:19). Do not acquiesce!

There is a famous quote that has probably been skewed over time. Mike Tyson is credited with saying, "Everybody has a plan until they get punched in the mouth."[3] Two thousand years ago the King of Heaven crashed into this world and "punched [Death] in the mouth" on several different fronts. This brawl involved poor people, religious leaders, a judicial system, and even the Devil himself. As rulers of this fallen world, Death and the Enemy had a plan until Jesus came and "punched [them] in the mouth." Those encounters comprise the content of this book.

---

[3] https://indygrit.community/blog/2019/2/9/everybody-has-a-plan-until-they-get-punched-in-the-mouth.

If you attend many funerals and discuss the life of the deceased with family and friends,

> *Mike Tyson is credited with saying, "Everybody has a plan until they get punched in the mouth."*

you will often hear how grateful they were that death finally came. They are grateful death relieved their departed loved ones from continued suffering. I understand their perspective, but may we never give credit to death. Death was never to be. It is a cruel fact of this fallen world due to *our* sin. May I never give credit to death!

No one in this fallen world could defeat Satan and death. None could ever return to whom they were created to be. All humankind lost forever what they once had. Songs long for it. Poets lament it. Tolkien writes, "The world has changed. I see it in the water. I feel it in the Earth. I smell it in the air. Much that once was is lost, for none now live who remember it."[4] We were created to live forever with God.

Yet the Word of God gives us the accounts of Jesus' insurrection against the ruler of this world and his formidable henchman, Death. We will look at

---

[4] Tolkien, J. R. R. *Lord of the Rings: Fellowship of the Ring.* DVD. Directed by Peter Jackson. Los Angeles: Warner Bros., 2001.

seven main arenas in which this fight took place: ignorance; human systems; illness; natural systems; the supernatural; Satan; and sin. In all honesty, the fight was not even close. Jesus beat Death like a drum.

DISCUSSION QUESTIONS

1. What are the ramifications of being created in the image of God? What difference does it make that He is a life-giving God?
2. Why do you think we tend to favor the long spans of life mentioned in Genesis rather than mourn the entrance of death into the world?
3. Have you heard of death getting credit for arriving to ease someone's suffering? Share. How do you feel about that?
4. Besides the seven arenas of death listed above, are there others you can think of in this fallen world?
5. Why might Jesus have come to fight death on several fronts before He defeated death through His own Crucifixion and Resurrection?

6. Read Acts 2:24. This is part of Peter's sermon on Pentecost. What does this statement mean to you? Why was it impossible?

Death, Life & Discipleship:

Ignorance

Death comes to humans in many forms. The ministry of Jesus as recorded in the Gospel of Mark makes it plain that Jesus focused on seven major approaches death uses. The first means of death we will cover is that of human ignorance—the lack of knowing and understanding who God is and what He has revealed. Jesus came to reveal Kingdom principles and the way Kingdom citizens are to think. Let us move right into the Word and we will begin to understand, know, and comprehend.

"They went to Capernaum, and when the Sabbath came, Jesus went into the synagogue and began to teach" (Mark 1:21).

"Once again Jesus went out beside the lake. A large crowd came to him, and he began to teach them" (Mark 2:13).

"When the Sabbath came, he began to teach in the synagogue, and many who heard him were amazed. "Where did this man get these things?" they asked. "What's this wisdom that has been given him?" (Mark 6:2).

"When Jesus landed and saw a large crowd, he had compassion on them, because they were like sheep without a shepherd. So, he began teaching them many things" (Mark 6:34).

We begin to see the priority of Jesus' ministry as He multiplies the good news throughout the region of Galilee. Teaching was Jesus' first instinct when entering a new location. This was because He understood that ignorance of God's Word led to death. Ironically, the one nation given the most revelation from God through the law and the prophets was still in deep need of clarity, illumination, and knowledge of the Word of God. In short, their spiritual ignorance caused death. Jesus, on the other hand, was bringing words of life to lift the veil and point the way so humans could thrive in this world and the next.

Clarity, understanding, truth, and reality are essential; especially in this life filled with dangers. Here is an example: you would do well not to hire me to implode a large building. I lack the knowledge. I am ignorant of how to accomplish the task. I would end up killing myself and probably a few others in the attempt. Ignorance kills, and it is no different in the spiritual realm than it is in the physical one. Religious pluralism has deadly eternal consequences. Wrong theology leads to building one's spiritual house on sand.

> *Clarity, understanding, truth, and reality are essential; especially in this life filled with dangers.*

Because of mankind's dire need to overcome ignorance, God spent over fifteen hundred years and used over forty authors to correct, illuminate, and erase man's lack of knowledge. He gave us the words of life to overcome death.

"Again Jesus began to teach by the lake. The crowd that gathered around him was so large that he got into a boat and sat in it out on the lake, while all the people were along

the shore at the water's edge. He taught them many things by parables, and in his teaching said: "Listen! A farmer went out to sow his seed. As he was scattering the seed, some fell along the path, and the birds came and ate it up. Some fell on rocky places, where it did not have much soil. It sprang up quickly, because the soil was shallow. But when the sun came up, the plants were scorched, and they withered because they had no root. Other seed fell among thorns, which grew up and choked the plants, so that they did not bear grain. Still other seed fell on good soil. It came up, grew and produced a crop, some multiplying thirty, some sixty, some a hundred times" (Mark 4:1-20 NIV).

A legitimate ruler has come into this world from Heaven to pour out on humankind understanding of how the Kingdom of God works. The only way Jesus' words hold any authority is if He Himself is speaking firsthand. Jesus knows what the Kingdom of God is like because He has come from the Kingdom of God. Consequently, He is the One who can explain the rules of the Kingdom. He is the One who knows the ins and outs of the Kingdom. This information has been lost since the perfect Garden vomited out its inhabitants. Jesus is telling the world how to get things back on track the way God designed them to be.

Disregarding or being ignorant of specific knowledge leads to problems. Every wife knows the results of a husband assembling a gift on Christmas Eve, without reading the directions. On a more serious note, in the spiritual world, a lack of knowing truth is one of death's ways of ensnaring people and drawing them in for a lethal bite. Jesus teaches life-giving messages on a variety of topics, but the lesson on the four soils will suffice in making the point.

PRINCIPLES FROM THE PASSAGE

The Sower is the teacher. The Sower tells the truths about how the Kingdom of God operates. The truth is illustrated as a seed. In this case, God is the Sower and God's Word is the seed. It is sown on four different soils and only one is receptive and fruitful. The soils represent people's hearts.

- Some people receive the teaching of God. Their knowledge is expanded, and they receive the teaching, thus promoting the Word of God. The problem is they let it sit there and do not apply it. Then Satan comes like a bird and plucks it away. What was life-transforming knowledge is now gone.

- Another type of person hears, gains knowledge, and receives the Word. But this person does not allow the teaching to penetrate and take root in their heart. Maybe the teaching was too hard for them or maybe it asked more than they were willing to give; but whatever the reason, they held it at arm's length and refused to let it go deep within their heart.

- The third type of person receives the truth but does not prioritize the Word. There are many things on their to-do list and the Word is only one of them. There are many things vying for their attention and the Word is lower on the priority totem pole than the other items.

- Keep in mind that in all these illustrations, the truth was not rejected but received initially. Jesus' teachings were heard and received. Jesus drew large groups of listeners in many regions. The Word of God is interesting, powerful, and effective, but as this parable demonstrates, it can be deemed of lesser importance by the receiver; it can be held at bay or ignored for a while.

- The last person of the story receives God's Word, and the result is a multiplication of life. What once

> *Nothing else takes first place, nothing else vies for their attention. The first focus of their lives is the Word of God.*

was dead is now made alive and reproduces. This person is found to be good soil. This person does four key things that are evidence that the Word of God has changed his/her level of knowledge, understanding, or ignorance. First, the person quickly receives the Word and does not let the enemy pluck it away. Second, the good soil allows the Word to penetrate deep into their soul where it can transform. Third, this person makes God's Word a priority. Nothing else takes first place, nothing else vies for their attention. The first focus of their lives is the Word of God. Finally, the word produces fruit in their life that is multiplied in others, sometimes thirty, sixty, or one hundred times or more!

Life has come to this person and it is visible. Ignoring, abandoning, building barriers, or devaluing the Word is at an end. They are wholly God's, and His Word is more valuable than diamonds.

Observing Mark 4:1-20 closer, we can pick up some more important principles to apply to our own lives. Notice the seed is sown everywhere. It is not given carefully or selectively. God's Word is to be shared everywhere we go. Sow it in good receptive places and even in places where it has no hope of taking root. Let it be a way of life. Testify to God's goodness, teach His principles, and share His Word with everyone. There is no worry of offending or anxiety over whether it is effective. May our lives be charitably extravagant in proclaiming God's Word and deeds. Leave the results to Him.

Death draws people in because of ignorance. This is true when a lack of accurate information can cause naval ships to collide, trains to derail, and planes to disappear. Confusion can lead to

> *Notice the seed is sown everywhere. It is not given carefully or selectively. God's Word is to be shared everywhere we go.*

death. If this is so, then why did Jesus teach in parables? That is too large of a subject for this chapter, but it is interesting to note that Jesus taught in parables and did not become frustrated when large groups became confused or just plain did not understand. Parables are like puzzles without a picture on a box to look at. They were presented once and that was it. However, Mark 4:33-34 gives us some solace. I have often wondered if Jesus knew or even cared if people did not understand the stories He told. You have probably wrestled with this in your own readings.

> *"With many such parables He was speaking the word to them, so far as they were able to hear it; ... But He was explaining everything privately to His own disciples."*

Jesus taught crowds at a level they could understand. The disciples asked questions, and Jesus explained the parables. The evidence of their acceptance of the parabolic instruction is seen in the fruit they bore. For the disciples, producing fruit took a little while because the Holy Spirit had not yet come.

The good news is if we have ears to hear then we can hear. The secrets of the Kingdom of God are available to everyone. Jesus came and, with relatable stories, revealed those secrets for all the world to see. Jesus is transparent. Jesus has nothing to hide. There is, however, a flip side to this coin. No encounter with the Word of God is neutral. There is no take-it or leave-it option. The Gospel truth is either positive for those who receive it and thus begin eternal life; or negative for those who reject it and consequently remain in death. Truth demands a response. It cannot be put on hold or squirreled away for a rainy day. It is always right to respond in obedience to God's Word immediately.

Ignorance of God's Word leads to death. That is one of the reasons the command to go make disciples is so important. Jesus is pictured as many things in the Bible. Here, and in passages like this, Jesus is the Master Teacher. He alone can bring words of life into a world of theological darkness and death. His words rob death of its power to veil knowledge and dull understanding. Because of Jesus' grace, we gain more understanding than our efforts of reading or listening deserve. We need to give priority time to studying the Bible. Knowledge, truth, and wisdom are found there.

Isaiah tells us the earth is full of the glory of God (Isaiah 6:3). Conversely, Jesus' ministry underscored that the earth was not full of God's knowledge. Jesus began defeating death by teaching of His Kingdom.

Everywhere Jesus taught, ignorance, lack of knowledge, wrong theology, and pagan belief were all overcome by a God-revealed understanding. Jesus won the battle between ignorance and Kingdom truth, and death was defeated. You need not fear death.

DISCUSSION QUESTIONS

1. How much of God's Word, God's truth, have you let lie and ignored by disregarding it and letting it fade away? How many messages have you heard, and left the church excited to have learned, only to have forgotten by the time kick-off comes around?

2. How can you allow/permit to God's Word to penetrate deep within your heart, your understanding, and your will? What practices could you implement to develop that lifestyle?

3. There are many places in God's Word where He tells us He must take priority, and even more than that, He is to have singularity. On a list of the most important things in your life,

His name should be the only name. Ask yourself, am I allowing anything ... *anything* to have a greater impact in/on my life than the Word of God?

4. We hate to think of how much time we have squandered on other things than God's Word. How much will you invest in listening to the Word of God? Remember He will give you more understanding than your listening deserves.

5. In general, the first act of Jesus when entering a new town or encountering a crowd was to teach them about the Kingdom of God and how it worked. Is this something we should model when we meet new people? Explain.

6. Do you sow the Word everywhere you go? Describe your methods. If your answer is no, what holds you back?

Death, Life & Discipleship

Human Systems

Another way death has weaseled its way into human life is through human systems. These systems—such as government and the judicial system—typically strive for beneficial results yet allow death to have its way in the human experience.

"So he immediately sent an executioner with orders to bring John's head. The man went, beheaded John in the prison, and brought back his head on a platter" (Mark 6:27-28).

Scripture tells us everyone is to submit themselves to the governing authorities (Romans

13:1). Why? Because God has established the institution of government. Nonetheless, these authorities—presided over by fallen women and men—become tools for selfish ends. All leaders have the opportunity to use their position to be selfless servants, however, most devolve into the basest figures and become a threat to those they govern.

Take a story like Mark 6:14-29. We see two human systems intersecting here: the governmental system and the legal system. The result is the death of John the Baptist. Was he a criminal? No. Was he a usurper to the throne of King Herod? No. We see abusive power exercised for a public leader's selfish benefit. King Herod is an out-of-control person who has deluded himself into believing he is in control. It is the picture of this world's bastardization of how government was meant to work. It is also a picture contrasting two kings. King Herod and King Jesus are diametrically opposed. King Herod is out of control. His human reign and rule led to death. Jesus—who in the previous chapters is shown to be in total control over storms, demons, and death—lives under the complete and total guidance of His Sovereign Father.

Herod's life, absent of the One who is in control, fails on multiple levels. Herod is influenced by the guilt of past unforgiven sin (Mark 6:14-16). Walk through this passage and notice:

- Herod is making decisions at a birthday party. Alcohol likely played a role and had control (6:21).
- John the Baptist, God's prophet, accused Herod of living an adulterous life. This would also cause Herod to feel he is not in control (6:17-18).
- Herodias was controlled by a vengeful bitterness toward John because John had called Herod out on his sinful marriage to her. She, in turn, manipulated and controlled Herod to bring about John's death (6:18-19, 24).
- Lust entered as another influencer, pulling the strings of the king. He allowed his flesh to rule him (6:22).
- Pride is another controller. Boastfully, Herod made a promise he soon regretted. He offered half of the kingdom to the daughter of Herodias. Once she made her request known, his pride precluded a retreat.

- Peer pressure could also be a factor. His guests looked on and pondered, "Will Herod keep his word?" (6:23-26)

Afraid of his guest's opinions, this king is not in charge at all. He is being bandied about by death's minions. Furthermore, he is giving a deaf ear to the call of his heart ...

"Herod feared John and protected him, knowing him to be a righteous and holy man" (Mark 6:20).

Death can identify a superior Master, such as conscience, even if it lurks within an incompetent governmental ruler or an inept judge. Could it prevail over a righteous and holy man? Yes! There are human systems in place that threaten everyone, even the righteous. This was death through the decisions of a weak mind and a leader absent of character or principle who used power, laws, and culture as a child uses tirades, tears, and tantrums to achieve their goal. Death had to act quickly, and John's head was removed, and his disciples carried away his body.

As alluded to above, the author of the Gospel is drawing a contrast between two kings: one heavenly and one earthly. Because we know the rest of the story, we know there can be godly women and men who head up human systems of local, state, and national governance. Human systems—like law enforcement, religion, the military, and medicine—can all be used improperly and lead to the death of human beings. They can also be used properly to save and promote life.

Be aware that human systems can be used to derail believers and even seemingly entrap the Son of God. Politics and religion were joined in Matthew 22:15-22 to seal the fate of Jesus. Yet again, Jesus gave God's established positions their due and *"...render[ed] unto Caesar what is Caesar's,"* but far more importantly, *"to God what is God's."*

The greatest story in which death uses human systems, Jesus' Crucifixion, is an emotional part of the greatest story ever told. Jesus went through the established authorities God the Father had put in place. Jesus was falsely accused. Jesus was unfairly interrogated. Jesus was wrongly condemned. Jesus was brutally executed. At this point, it seemed as if earthly kings were superior to the Heavenly King.

Yet, we and the disciples know that Jesus, King of Life, conquered death. Jesus had the last word. Jesus overcame death by human systems to provide life for all—even those who murdered Him. Come to Him by faith. *"This is the victory that has overcome the world—our faith"* (1 John 5:4). Death is insatiable. Death is graceless. God, by grace, redeemed the world by overcoming fallen human systems, headed up by fallen humans, to provide a perfect salvation to all who believe and answer the call, *"Follow Me"* (Mark 1:17).

A legitimate Governor from Heaven had come to earth and walked among us. As with Herod's and even Caesar's rule, it shook earthly governments to their core. This is evidenced throughout history as Christianity called out those who use their positions of power in an ungodly and unscriptural manner. There is no shortage of self-centered rulers who end up doing the bidding of death. Death used Stalin, Hitler, Pol Pot, Xi Jinping, Kim Jong-un, and many others.

Jesus came from the Kingdom of Life and struck a staggering blow to the jaw of human systems, led by fallen, unrepentant humans. He will one day return and reign in power and authority over all the world, thereby bringing glory to the Father. We are given some pictures of what righteousness in office looks like.

"For a child will be born to us, a son will be given to us;

And the government will rest on His shoulders;

And His name will be called Wonderful Counselor, Mighty God, Eternal Father, Prince of Peace" (Isaiah 9:6).

And Isaiah again prophesies a coming ruler:

"...The Spirit of the Lord will rest on Him,

The spirit of wisdom and under-standing,

The spirit of counsel and strength,

The spirit of knowledge and the fear of the LORD.

And He will delight in the fear of the LORD,

And He will not judge by what His eyes see,

Nor make a decision by what His ears hear;

But with righteousness He will judge the poor,

And decide with fairness for the afflicted of the earth;

And He will strike the earth with the rod of His mouth,

And with the breath of His lips He will slay the wicked.

Also righteousness will be the belt about His loins,

And faithfulness the belt about His waist" (Isaiah 11:2-5).

This is the template for human systems, so death cannot have its way in this world. This is the model to shoot for even if it is not achieved, which it will not be until His return. The problem is those heading up our human systems do not even know of this template, nor do they care to know it. It would confine them, bind them, restrict them, and, after all, they believe that they know better than He!

To narrow a choice of governance to communism, socialism, or democratic republicanism is to leave out the greatest form of governance of all. The governance of a God of perfect love, living and ruling in the hearts of all. Where do I sign up? Where can I become a citizen of the Kingdom of Heaven? Follow Jesus! Come by Faith.

PRINCIPLES FROM THE PASSAGE

As is true with most rulers or people who have positions of authority, rivals are rarely befriended, and few are tolerated. Whether it's Saul and David, Herod and John, or Caiaphas and Jesus;

those who rock the boat are seen as enemies. Those who bring the flame that exposes the flaws are snuffed out.

- The message of Jesus draws attention, and those who are messengers of Jesus are often seen as inconvenient to have around. It can result in broken friendships, broken bones, or even death.
- Our past sinful choices hang around like ghosts and can only be exorcised through the forgiveness provided by Jesus. Herod believed his past had come back to haunt him in the form of Jesus.
- People falsely believe they are in control of their lives. Things like status, philosophy, finances, friends, and even theology can support this false view of self-control. Dealing with this reality through full surrender to the One who is in control is the only answer.
- Those heading up human systems are frail, broken, and fallen people. Do not expect them to do what only God can do.
- Ungodly leaders inevitably bring about chaos rather than peace, sorrow rather than joy, death rather than life. Only the Prince of Life

can promise and provide. It is imperative to place godly people in positions of authority in human systems. This is not because they are superior leaders; it is because they have surrendered to the One who is.

> *Human systems, however well-intentioned, can lead to death.*

Remember, God's design for human systems is not bad. It is the quality of the character of the person in charge that makes the difference. Need a good magistrate? Find the one who has surrendered to the greatest Magistrate of all. Need a good CEO? Find the one who has surrendered to the greatest CEO.

Human systems, however well-intentioned, can lead to death. Systems—like utilities, traffic control, medicine, government, military, and even disaster relief—operated by a fallen human element can lead to human death. Sovereign Jesus is never out of control. He modeled mastery over death even before eternally defeating death on the cross. You need not fear death.

DISCUSSION QUESTIONS

1. Have you ever done something in the past that came back to haunt you? Explain. Did it have lasting effects?
2. Was Herod a king with a good heart who just let circumstances get out of control? Why or why not?
3. Herod's problem was that he did not know who Jesus was. Do you know, and does it shape how you relate to other human beings? If so, share how.
4. Would you say your experience with human systems has been positive or negative? Explain.
5. Herod was controlled by ego, public opinion, accountability to others, protection of position, social power, lust, and the leverage of a spouse. Which of these are you most susceptible to? Why?
6. The previous chapters in Mark show Jesus in perfect control: ministering, healing, preaching, teaching, calming a storm, raising the dead, and casting out demons. This chapter describes a king who is out of control.

Why? What is the point Mark is trying to make?

Death, Life & Discipleship

Illness & Disease

According to Matthew 4:23, Jesus' ministry consisted of teaching, preaching, and healing. Healing is necessary in a fallen world. A lack of healing leads to death. Jesus warred against sickness and disease throughout His ministry. He healed Peter's mother-in-law. He healed lepers. He healed paralytics and gave sight to the blind. Left unattended, illness and disease lead human beings into death's waiting arms.

There is no evidence of any illness or disease Jesus could not completely heal. The Kingdom He brings is a Kingdom of wholeness, health, and life, which triumphs over all handicaps, diseases, and death. Because there are so many episodes in this story, I will select only a few for the sake of time.

> *"A woman who had had a hemorrhage for twelve years, and had endured much at the hands of many physicians, and had spent all that she had and was not helped at all, but rather had grown worse – after hearing about Jesus, she came up in the crowd behind Him and touched His cloak. For she thought, 'If I just touch His garments, I will get well.' Immediately the flow of her blood was dried up; and she felt in her body that she was healed of her affliction"* (Mark 5:25-34).

> *She knew that to simply touch Jesus was enough to be healed.*

Death has no mercy. The trajectory of this woman's life was on the downward slope. For twelve years, she had endured inept physicians, squandered all her money on ineffective treatments, and had progressively grown worse. Enter the Great Physician. To have the faith to go to Him was enough to be healed. All the reasonable, logical, culturally acceptable cures had been tried. With no other option, an unbeliever took a chance on Jesus and found life.

Something to keep in mind as we read this account is the Old Testament law, which stipulates that a woman with a bleeding issue was unable to participate in worship with the community of God (Leviticus 15:19, 25). Because of her bleeding, she had been perpetually unclean for the past twelve years and had been excluded from the public worship of Yahweh with family, relatives, and friends. She was a spiritual outcast.

Likewise, keep in mind that the bleeding made her unclean, and an unclean person had to announce that they were unclean. So, for the past twelve years, she had made it known to all who would listen that she was unclean and, therefore, unfit to join the people of God. This public pronunciation made everyone aware so they would stay away and not become unclean. In our passage, we see that she took a chance. She joined the crowd. She latched on to Jesus and found healing. Death was defeated once again before Jesus ever made it to the cross. Her passionate, hopeful pursuit of Jesus brought her new life.

Jesus healed many lepers. Mark 1:40-42 is another example of Jesus overcoming Death by healing one pleading for Jesus to act.

"And a leper came to Jesus, beseeching Him and falling on his knees before Him, and saying, 'If You are willing, You can make me clean.' Moved with compassion, Jesus stretched out His hand and touched him, and said to him, 'I am willing; be cleansed.' Immediately the leprosy left him and he was cleansed."

In Jesus' day, to receive news from the priest that you had leprosy was tantamount to hearing you have stage four cancer and that it has metastasized from your lungs to your lymph nodes and into your bone marrow. I am sure they received a broken-hearted look from the priest and a shake of the head followed by, "There is nothing more we can do."

Today, leprosy is a curable disease, and we can contrast these stories with our more modern understanding of science and medicine. Jesus knew the seriousness of disease during His campaign on earth. He knew the ramifications if leprosy was left untreated. Death had penetrated humanity comprehensively. But when Jesus entered the picture, death lost its hold because the Divine Son of God wrenched the sick, the disabled, and the diseased out of death's grip and into wellness, health, and abundant living. Facing illness and disease head-on, Jesus defeated this tool of death.

I will elaborate a little on the Old Testament elements in this story. The discharges that kept either a man or woman from joining the fellowship of believers in worship had to do with the reproduction of life (Lev. 15). To expel

> *God provided a means of being restored to a living community, and a way to no longer be representative of unfruitfulness.*

from one's body the fluid or the egg that it joins with was not representative of the people of God. In other words, these biological events were representative of sterility, unfruitfulness, and death, not fruitfulness and life.

God was not rejecting the person but the picture. He loved the person but not what his or her body conveyed to the community of life. He provided a means through the Law for that person to be restored to the community. It came in the forms of washings, a time of separating oneself, sacrificing prescribed offerings, and the like.

Now, let me move a little further into the understanding that illness is an instrument used by death to take a person's life. A rhetorical structure is used in this story of the woman with the bleeding issue. Intercalation is used here. One story is being interrupted—the story of Jairus' daughter—while the story of the woman with the bleeding issue is told. Then, the author returns to finish the story of Jesus raising the little girl from the dead.

Mark 5:21-24 informs the reader that a synagogue official's daughter is at the point of death. By faith, the father pleads, *"Please come and lay Your hands on her, so that she will get well and live."* The father knew to whom to go. The father had confidence Jesus could cure her. The father knew of Jesus' reputation for providing life, conquering illness, and preventing death.

After the story of the hemorrhaging woman, we return to the story of Jairus' daughter.

"While He was still speaking, they came from the house of the synagogue official, saying, 'Your daughter has died; why trouble the Teacher anymore?' But Jesus overhearing

what was being spoken, said to the synagogue official, 'Do not be afraid any longer, only believe'" (Mark 5:35-36).

The folks that came from the house believed there was no further need to trouble Jesus. They believed He could heal illness, sickness, and disease. But this girl had died! They did not believe Jesus could raise a dead person to life. They were confident in Jesus but not *that* confident. Only God could do that! They were ready to send Jesus on His way. The people's understanding at this point was that Jesus' power, amazing as it was, only addressed the illnesses of humankind.

> *Illness can be reversed to health, and even death can be reversed to life.*

No one can come back from the dead! Or can they? Mark describes Jesus as Lord, not only over all sickness and disease but also over illnesses that lead to death. He is undaunted by death. This King of Heaven pursues the person and steals them back out of the jaws of death.

Death takes a beating on two accounts in this story. Illness can be reversed to health, and even death can be reversed to life. This happens without conjuring up spells, potions, confronting oracles, or consulting the dead. Make note of how easily Jesus raises the little girl.

"Taking the child by the hand, He said to her, 'Talitha kum!' (which translated means, "Little girl, I say to you, get up!") (Mark 6:41).

Without breaking a sweat Jesus calmly and simply speaks her into life. Keep that in mind when folks tell you complex details of prayer, healing, or spiritual warfare at conferences. Paganism is complicated. The Kingdom of God is simple. If you leave confused with a long list of things to do, ask God again if what you just heard was of Him.

So, what is the effect? When Jesus heals from illness to life, or from death to life, how much recovery time is needed? This twelve-year-old hops up and gets back to life. Death could not hold her if Jesus were her Physician. Now, that is not saying she did not grow old and eventually die. However, in this case, she lived and died and lived again and died again. I suspect that after what Jesus had done for her, she lives eternally.

PRINCIPLES FROM THE PASSAGE

- God initiates the process and removes the barriers to being a part of His family or a part of the community of Jesus' followers. Thank You, Jesus!
- To encounter Jesus is to be changed. You cannot encounter the Living God and not be changed by that encounter. The woman simply touched what was attached to Jesus (i.e., His garment) and was forever changed. As followers of Jesus, we are attached to Jesus and can be change agents for others trying to find Him.
- Jairus and this woman were at opposite ends of Jewish society. Jairus was a leader and influencer in the community. The woman was an impoverished and unclean outcast. It did not matter to Jesus. Jesus healed all who came to Him.
- Both stories show people doing whatever it took to get to Jesus and ask him to help.

Jesus had no problem defeating death caused by illness, disability, and disease. He made the mute speak, the blind see, and the leper healthy. Jesus defeated death through healing. You need not fear death.

DISCUSSION QUESTIONS

1. Have you ever prayed for the healing of someone, but physical healing never came? Expound on your insights and feelings as you worked through this event.

2. Do you think Jesus is modeling healing and resurrection for His disciples so they can imitate Him? Or is Jesus performing healings and resurrection to reveal who He is to a puzzled group of Jewish followers? What difference does it make? Explain.

3. Read James 5:13-16. Do you have the confidence James has? Why or why not?

4. In Mark 5:21-43, you have a story about a synagogue ruler who would most likely be a respected member of the worshiping community. You also have the story of a woman who is a bankrupt outcast, excluded from the worshiping community. What does this tell you

about Jesus and how He views those in need? What is God saying to you through this?

5. Both people's lives were in chaos. Jesus brought peace to both with His words and His actions. Do you know of someone in chaos who needs to find peace? What can you say? What can you do?

6. Jesus called the healed woman "daughter." Jairus' daughter was tenderly raised up by Jesus. Does the term *daughter* have any significance in these stories? Share.

Death, Life & Discipleship:

Natural Systems

"On that day, when evening came, He said to them, 'Let us go over to the other side.' Leaving the crowd, they took Him along with them in the boat, just as he was; and the other boats were with Him. And there arose a fierce gale of wind, and the waves were breaking over the boat so much that the boat was already filling up. Jesus Himself was in the stern, asleep on the cushion; and they woke Him and said to Him, 'Teacher, do You not care that we are perishing?' And He got up and rebuked the wind and said to the sea, 'Hush, be still.' And the wind died down and it *became perfectly calm. And He said to them, 'Why are you afraid? Do you still have no faith? They became very much afraid and said to one another, 'Who then is this, that even the wind and the sea obey Him?'"* (Mark 4:35-41).

Fallen creation has an uncanny way of taking human life. This is such a common occurrence that people often designate death through natural disasters as "acts of God." In 2004, an Indian Ocean earthquake caused a tsunami that killed 230,000 people.[5] Then, in 2010, an earthquake in Haiti added 315,000 to the death toll caused by natural calamity.[6] In fact, so many people die in floods, it is hard to accurately list the dead. In 1931 alone, the flooding in China took anywhere from 400,000 to 4,000,000 souls.[7] Death loves a natural disaster.

---

[5] Editors, History.com. "Tsunami devastates Indian Ocean coast." *This Day In History,* A & E Television Networks, 13 Nov. 2009, this-day-in-history/tsunami-devastates-indian-ocean-coast, Accessed 7 May 2020.

[6] H. Kit Miyamoto, csengineermag.com. "The Earthquake That Killed 315,000 People." *Civil + Structural Engineer Media,* Zweig Group, 1 Jan. 2020, csengineermag.com/the-earthquake-that-killed-315000-people. Accessed 30 April 2020.

[7] Wikipedia.org. "1931 China Floods." 4 May 2020. Wikipedia en.wikipedia.org/wiki/1931_China_floods. Accessed 2 May 2020.

It seems like nature has an unending appetite for turning life into death. This was true in the first century and is still true today. Nothing has changed. Just like people in Jesus' day, we can still die from floods, fire, earthquakes, tornadoes, hurricanes, tsunamis, avalanches, mudslides, and volcanoes.

In this passage, Mark describes Jesus calming the storm. This is considered one of Jesus' super-miracles. This miracle was beyond what was thought possible, even for the Messiah. Mark includes this super miracle in Chapter Four to drive home the point of Jesus' ability to control nature. This illustrates Jesus' divinity and power to the Roman reader. Mark depicts Jesus changing weather patterns, casting out at least two thousand demons, and raising the dead. The original reader's question would be, "Can Caesar do that?" Jesus and Caesar both claimed to be divine. Jesus, however, proved He was divine through miracles.

Calming a storm is done amid chaos. It involves conditions beyond human control. Nature is bigger than us. It is like a bully randomly and sporadically deciding to pick on us, and there is nothing we can do about it. Through the chaos of natural disasters, we see how helpless we truly are. Likewise, we are reminded that we live in a fallen world.

Furthermore, this is another time we are told the disciples were afraid or terrified and pondered, "Who is this guy?" The reason for this is they do not yet understand the Messiah to be a weather-pattern-changer; only God Himself could do that! Jesus was not conforming to their preconceived idea of a Messiah. Jesus effortlessly took on death caused by natural systems. How hard was it? Jesus was so unconcerned about death winning this bout He was asleep in the stern.

Rembrandt van Rijn portrays this story beautifully in his painting *The Storm on the Sea of Galilee.*[8] In this picture, some of the disciples are clearly frantic, and one disciple is so nauseated he is vomiting over the side. On the other hand, the disciples who are closest to Jesus in the stern appear much calmer; they seem to be inquiring of Jesus rather than panicking. Those farthest from Jesus' presence are pictured trying to get ahead of Jesus and solve the problem themselves. Mark's audience is simply to read, marvel at the power

> *His reign is full, comprehensive, and complete.*

[8] Van Rijn, Rembrandt. *Christ In The Storm On The Sea Of Galilee.* 1633. The Isabella Stewart Gardner Museum, Boston. www.gardnermuseum.org/ experience/collection/ 10953#gref. Accessed 22 Apr. 2020.

Christ displayed, and be amazed that nature had no sway over our Savior. The Creator was in the boat with them. Death had no chance that day when it came against Jesus' disciples. With its weapons of a fallen creation, Death could not win. Death could not kill. Death could not even sink the boat. The Captain of Life was aboard and commanded the wind and the waves. They listened to His Sovereign command, *"Hush, be still."*

I do not know if you can imagine a perfect calm, but that resulted from His command. There were other boats out there that could verify the disciple's account of what happened. We do not just have to take the disciples' word for it. The waves could have subsided over time, say an hour or so. The waves could have become less severe at His authoritative order. No, that is not how Jesus demonstrated His reign over death. The wind relented, and the calm that resulted was instantly perfect.

Jesus modeled to His disciples no anxiety, fear, or abandoning their mission. They are on their voyage to "the other side" of the sea. Nothing can stand in the way of God's mission and purpose being realized in His incarnate Son. Jesus fully trusted God's will to accomplish His goal through Him, so why worry? A parallel can be drawn from this story. The peace in

Jesus and the supernatural calm of the sea exceeds the level of chaos Jesus and His disciples were pitted against.

Let us not miss some of the details of this story. This is an exhausted group of disciples who have been involved in non-stop ministry. This rag-tag group of men are like drowned rats headed to the Gentile side of the sea. They are leaving their comfort zone of the land they know, and under cover of night, they are heading into the spiritual darkness of secular, pagan shores. Tired, frightened, and wet to the bone, this war with natural systems was only the Enemy's first offense. They are heading for a storm of biblical proportions in the spiritual realm when they arrive at the other side.

While leading a men's group for a few years, we studied several topics, took on a few challenges, and even began an annual conference. Yet, most of what we did was theoretical and conducted within the church walls. I introduced them to the idea of going door to door in one of our local villages as we surveyed the people on what type of church they were looking for. Our intention was to gain insight about our local church. We would get face-to-face feedback from village residents and hear their opinions. But more importantly, these men would move out of their comfort zones and outside the church walls. They would knock on strangers' doors and speak to people they did not know face to face. You know what? They did it!

Over the years, one result that came from this interaction was that some of the men moved their families into that community to influence the villagers through being their actual neighbors. A group of around eight families decided to be on a mission together to make disciples in this hamlet. There is now a Christian school, a food bank, and a handyman/woman service. There is also ongoing care for the elderly and widows, small group Bible studies in low-income apartments, movies in the park, and community cookouts. This is a missional community led by the Spirit reaching out to a lost world. When God moves us out of our comfort zone into dangerous waters, something beautiful happens because He is with us. Life wins.

PRINCIPLES FROM THE PASSAGE

- Regardless of the situation we find ourselves in, with Jesus, there is never an end of hope.

- God often responds when we come to the end of ourselves and our plans.

- We often get exasperated at God for not automatically caring for us in times of trouble. God wants us to come to Him in times of trouble and request help. We can make that request early or late in whatever scenario we find ourselves. We sometimes find ourselves in life-threatening situations through no fault of our own.

- God does care. He is with you in the storm. He may calm the storm and bring perfect peace. He will ride through the storm with you, but you may think He is asleep.

- Nature will often throw many potentially life-threatening events our way. Make sure Jesus is in the boat.

- Jesus being in the boat of the disciples also brought peace to all the other boats on the lake. They were blessed because of Jesus' work with His disciples.

- Faith and fear do not go together. If you have faith, let it conquer your fear. If you fear, do not allow it to conquer your faith.

- Like the disciples, there will be times when Jesus does things we do not expect. Give Jesus free rein. He's God and He can do whatever He wants in our lives in any way He wants to do it.

- Sometimes, you move your disciples out into unknown and threatening territory. As a disciple-maker, you lead them out into uncharted waters—out of their comfort zone—in order to stretch their faith and help them move into a deeper dependency and faith in Jesus.

Jesus has the power to change natural events. In doing so, He defeats death. Death uses the natural occurrences of a young, fallen earth in order to feed the grave. Jesus easily overcomes these tragedies. You need not fear death.

DISCUSSION QUESTIONS

1. Have you ever found yourself in a life-threatening storm? How did you react?

2. We are often hard on the disciples' behavior, but how do you think you would have reacted

to the storm? What do you make of Jesus being seemingly without a care?

3. Do you think the disciples were more fearful of the storm or the power of Jesus?

4. Mark focuses on Jesus' identity in Chapters 1-8. How does this story help the reader know more of Jesus' identity? How does it help the reader learn more about the disciples?

5. Jesus is taking His disciples through a storm at night to an unclean and spiritually dark Gentile land. Why leave the comfort of their Jewish homeland? Why not at least wait and head out in the morning?

6. In this scenario, Jesus defeats death by His authority and power over nature. Which is more impressive to you: Jesus defeating ignorance, Jesus defeating human systems, Jesus defeating illness, or Jesus defeating nature? Explain.

Death, Life & Discipleship

Supernatural World

Jesus gave His disciples authority to minister just as He ministered. According to Matthew's account, Jesus' main ministries were teaching, preaching, and healing. In partnership with these three, is an ongoing knock-down drag-out brawl with the supernatural world. This is a very real, unseen world, a historically recorded world that battled against Jesus and sought to work stealthily in partnership with death.

Jews of Jesus' day clearly believed in a supernatural world that was at odds with God, and that sought to live in defiance of the way God created the world to operate. Satan is the head of this realm, and he will be the focus of our next chapter. This chapter will focus mainly on demonic activity. Demons sought the destruction of human beings through any means necessary. They were fully aware of who Jesus was and that He had come from Heaven into their realm. They knew this Son of the Most High was beginning an insurrection that would topple their influence and their ability to detrimentally affect earthly beings.

The Apostle James makes a clear pronouncement concerning their knowledge of Jesus in 2:19, *"You believe that there is one God. Good! Even the demons believe that – and shudder"* (NIV). The demonic world is not ignorant of God, His word, His plans, or His purposes for humankind. The Gospel of Mark highlights several interactions Jesus had with demons. For instance, Jesus called one out in the middle of a synagogue service.

"They went into Capernaum; and immediately on the Sabbath He entered the synagogue and began to teach. They were amazed at His teaching; for He was teaching them as one having authority, and not as the scribes. Just then there was a man in their synagogue with an unclean spirit; and he

cried out, saying 'What business do we have with each other, Jesus of Nazareth? Have you come to destroy us? I know who You are – the Holy One of God!' And Jesus rebuked him, saying, 'Be quiet, and come out of him!' Throwing him into convulsions, the unclean spirit cried out with a loud voice and came out of him. They were all amazed, so that they debated among themselves, saying, 'What is this? A new teaching with authority! He commands even the unclean spirits, and they obey Him'" (Mark 1:21-27).

Imagine attending a church service at which a member is called out by Jesus because he/she is a vessel for demonic possession! How long had this person been attending? Did anyone notice? Did anyone pick up on

> *"What is this? A new teaching with authority! He commands even the unclean spirits, and they obey Him" (Mark 1:21-27).*

the unclean speech? Did anyone pick up on the ungodly lifestyle? If this individual had not called out Jesus, it seems the people of God would have never called him out.

Mark makes an interesting revelation. First, the Trinity obviously knows who Jesus is: *"You are My beloved Son, in You I am well-pleased"* (Mark 1:11). Second, from the passage above and many others throughout the Gospel, we know the supernatural world has a clear picture of who Jesus is. The demonic world is clearly cognizant of Christ's identity. However, as we move through the book, Jesus often remains a mystery to the disciples. Sometimes, they seem to get it, and other times, they do not. The crowds, along with the religious leaders, do not recognize Him for who He is either.

Death had its way for millennia until Jesus showed up on the scene. The demons are another tool for the destruction of human life, and Jesus has come to put a stop to it. The Kingdom of Life has entered to conquer the Kingdom of Darkness. Again, Jesus does not break a sweat defeating these supernatural beings.

As a young boy, my friends would join me on a journey to the "8th Street graveyard," properly named *Moss Cemetery*. It was a short walk from our neighborhood. Usually, it was at night. Usually, it was during autumn. The bright moon lit up the Indiana night. There was a chill in the air, and the wind was just enough to stir the leaves across the fading graves. The graveyard was no longer open for burials. Time and weather had had their influence, and many headstones were no longer decipherable.

Chapter 5 of Mark reminds me of those times. Mark, usually concise and sparse in his storytelling, lends the first twenty verses to the disciples' own graveyard story. This is the rest of the story following the night Jesus calmed the storm. Keep in mind the disciples are already spooked.

"They came to the other side of the sea, into the country of the Gerasenes. When He got out of the boat, immediately a man from the tombs with an unclean spirit met Him, and he had his dwelling among the tombs. And no one was able to bind him anymore, even with a chain; because he had often been bound with shackles and chains, and the chains had been torn apart by him and the shackles broken in pieces, and no one was strong enough to subdue him" (Mark 5:1-4).

This wretched man is living with the dead. This is an apt picture of the result of death using demons to carry out its goal. Make no mistake: demons seek the death of those they torment. Illness can linger, but unchecked, its goal is a slow, agonizing death.

Demons are often the same way. Death is not kind. Death is not compassionate. This man, who later we are told was unsound of mind and physically injured, would soon be numbered among the tombs.

> *"Constantly, night and day, he was screaming among the tombs and in the mountains, and gashing himself with stones. Seeing Jesus from a distance, he ran up and bowed down before Him; and shouting with a loud voice, he said, 'What business do we have with each other, Jesus, Son of the Most High God? I implore You by God, do not torment me!'"* (Mark 5:5-7).

He is constantly screaming and cutting himself as he wanders among the graves, exposed to the elements. Again, the disciples and Jesus had ministered non-stop for an extremely long time; they rowed for hours fighting a storm; left comfort, and entered terror, all for one guy. This man is out of his mind and possessed by at least two thousand demons. What lengths Jesus goes to to save just one! The urgency Jesus displays to heal this man may indicate that this poor soul was not long for this world. He had been among the tombs for a considerable time. His neighbors had besieged him. Death and the demons were about to win again until Jesus showed up to punch a legion of demons in the face and end this man's torture.

Jesus asked the man's name, and the demons responded, *"My name is Legion; for we are many"* (Mark 5:9). A legion of soldiers in the Roman army ranged anywhere from two thousand to six thousand.[9] The use of the term "legion" and the number of swine support the idea that Jesus is not battling a demon or two. The Son of the Most High God is about to easily dispose of at least two thousand demons from one man.

What kind of life would we have to live so that we would make a comfortable home for two thousand demons to reside in us? One demon in a synagogue pale in comparison to this scenario. This is the pagan "other side" of the lake, full of witchcraft, sorcery, and demonic spirits.

> *Death and the demons were about to win again until Jesus showed up to punch a legion of demons in the face and end this man's torture.*

9 Truman, C. N. "The Roman Army And Warfare." www.historylearningsite.co.uk/ancient-rome/the-roman-army-and-warfare/. Accessed 7 May 2020.

Yet that is where Jesus took His disciples. It is interesting and humorous to note that the disciples seem to be only observers in this story.

So, is Jesus effective in His endeavor to save the man of the tombs?

"They ... observed the man who had been demon-possessed sitting down, clothed and in his right mind, the very man who had had the 'legion'" (Mark 5:15).

Jesus had completely restored the man. No longer was he under the control of the supernatural world and the bidding of demons. No longer was he exposed to the elements naked and screaming. Jesus had defeated the supernatural world soundly and unquestionably. Death was defeated once more.

As I pass by any cemetery today, I sigh a little. When I see all the gravestones, I do not focus on death. I imagine life without death. A cemetery is a reminder of the devastation of death. Oh, the loss of knowledge that lies beneath. The wonder and impact of all the life experiences that are no more; the joy that has vanished. Life has been stolen along with amazing skills, experience, and wisdom. Every life lost leaves a hole in the mosaic of humankind. What a calamity has befallen us because of our choice to live in defiance of the way God designed the world.

PRINCIPLES FROM THE PASSAGE

- It is highly likely that there are people in your congregation who are living Christ-opposed lives. It may even be you.
- Regardless of the hardship, Jesus pursued saving lost people and modeled that lifestyle for His disciples. Barriers such as lack of sleep, spiritual warfare, danger, and exhaustion were not obstacles that prevented Him from seeking and saving the lost.
- Jesus went to a world that embraced death. On several occasions, He headed straight into a world that was opposed to life and defiant toward God.
- Jesus, not the disciples, is the authority who takes on the supernatural world. In this story, the disciples are not involved in casting out Legion. There is a time for training and equipping, and not prematurely pushing your disciples out into the battle, a time for them to simply observe.

- The restoration of the mind happens when one encounters Jesus and is transformed through the encounter.

- A desire to follow Jesus is the outcome of justification. This can happen regardless of how "bad" we are. If Jesus can save someone who was so evil, one who hosted thousands of demons, He can save anyone.

- A desire to obey and go tell the world what Jesus has done for you is a result of becoming a new creation in Christ.

- In general, people do not want you to shake up their world and the status quo. Change makes them feel unsafe and out of control. Living in darkness blinds people to the wonderful light of Jesus.

When you join the insurrection, you put a target on your back. But fear not! Jesus defeated death through demonic attack with overwhelming power, majesty, and authority. You need not fear death.

DISCUSSION QUESTIONS

1. Do you know some folks in your church body who have unclean spirits? Their speech proclaims Jesus, but their life does not produce

eternal fruit. The topics they focus on are not Kingdom-minded but earthly-minded. Does self-centeredness give them away? *This is not a time to name names,* and I may be describing you. Why not pray right now for the person on your heart to embrace full surrender to the authority of Jesus?

2. Did you think you were too sinful for Jesus to forgive you? Do you still think that? Why or why not? Explain.

3. Why do you think the disciples are absent from this story of the demon-possessed man in the graveyard on a stormy night? How do you think you would have responded in that situation?

4. The supernatural world knows who Jesus is (v.7). Why do you think Jesus asked this man his name (v.9)? Did Jesus not know His name?

5. Is Jesus bartering with the demons (v.12-13)? Is He deceiving them or outsmarting them? Why do they need a vessel to enter?

6. This seems like a wonderful deliverance. Yet, the people of the area want Jesus to go away (vs. 15-17). Why, after seeing a man transformed from death and darkness to life and light, would they not thank Jesus and ask Him to stay?

Death, Life & Discipleship:

Satan

Satan was defeated on the cross. When Jesus walked out of the tomb there was no chance of a do-over, no grounds for an appeal, no best-of-seven series. Yet there is a story in Mark that comes long before the blood-soaked wood and the rusty nails. It is a proclamation that is easy to miss. It is a picture of God some might not like. It is an expression of power that cannot be ignored.

Death and Satan are in cahoots, which means they are working together to accomplish a goal. Here is a story about a strong man—who is not quite strong enough—and his house.

"And He came home, and the crowd gathered again, to such an extent that they could not even eat a meal. When His own people heard of this, they went out to take custody of Him; for they were saying, 'He has lost His senses.' The scribes who came down from Jerusalem were saying, 'He is possessed by Beelzebul,' and 'He casts out the demons by the ruler of the demons.' And He called them to Himself and began speaking to them in parables, 'How can Satan cast out Satan? If a kingdom is divided against itself, that kingdom cannot stand. If a house is divided against itself, that house will not be able to stand. If Satan has risen up against himself and is divided, he cannot stand, but he is finished!" (Mark 3:20-26).

Jesus uses logic in confronting the religious leaders. Logic and reason would appeal to the ordinary spectator as well. These leaders have an agenda. The agenda is to deceive the common folks and turn them against Jesus, even if it means promoting nonsensical fallacies, they themselves know to be false. Jesus and His Kingdom teachings are becoming too popular.

The penal system and the mental health system, as well as addiction clinics, are full of self-opposed people. We've probably all heard the aphorism taken from this passage, "A house divided cannot stand." In addition to it being true of individuals, Jesus' statement illustrates that it is true about groups as well. Likewise, we see this truth played out among sports teams, dysfunctional families, marriages, political parties, churches, and nations. To be honest, Satan loves this.

Up to this point, Jesus had successfully cast out numerous demons. On this occasion, a sizeable crowd formed and followed Jesus from place to place. The religious leaders learned of this and came to see for themselves. Their initial reaction was to stifle this by claiming Jesus was empowered by the Devil. He was operating by Satan's power! Keep in mind that the readers have already been informed Jesus' power is from the Holy Spirit who descended upon Him at His baptism. This means the Jewish leaders are fraudulently claiming that Jesus is empowered by Satan and not the Holy Spirit.

Beelzebub and Beelzebul are two names for the same person: Satan. Nonetheless, this passage uses the name Beelzebul. This appellation means *lord of the house*. This is why Jesus' illustration is of a house divided. Notice the three arenas Jesus mentions. A kingdom divided, then a house divided, and then Satan divided. Satan has a *kingdom,* and we were once in it. Satan has a *house,* and we were once in it. Satan is a ruler within the supernatural world and this world. This is a startling truth.

But fear not! Look at verse twenty-seven. This is where Satan takes a beatin'; and keep in mind Beelzebul is the strong man of the house.

"But no one can enter the strong man's house and plunder his property unless he first binds the strongman, and then he will plunder his house."

Satan is the ruler of this world, and his properties are the people of this world. Another subtle point Jesus is making is Satan's house *will* get plundered. Hallelujah!

Do not miss the picture above. Jesus, a King of another Kingdom, has entered the realm of the strong man's kingdom like a burglar or robber, a thief in the night. Jesus is wants to carry off Satan's property (i.e., people), Jesus steals the people of Satan's kingdom. He does it in a covert insurrection. In the Gospels, Jesus does this all the time. Satan, hoping to bring death to people, has begun to lose the battle. A Stronger King has infiltrated and is winning subjects over to His Kingdom every time He encounters Satan's minions. Satan is strong. Jesus is stronger.

The lord of the house will be bound at the cross—though he does not know it. Jesus, a superior foe, will defeat Satan, rob him of his property, and enrich His own Kingdom with folks brought from death to life. Again, God is simply doing what He has said He will do. God said He would act in Isaiah 42:7, *"... to open eyes that are blind, to free captives from prison and release from the dungeon those who sit in darkness."*

And again, in Psalm 102: 19-20:

> *"The LORD looked down from his sanctuary on high, from heaven he viewed the earth, to hear the groans of the prisoners and release those condemned to death."*

Likewise, Psalm 68:18-20 proclaims:

> *"When you ascended on high, you led captives in your train; you received gifts from men, even from the rebellious – that you, O LORD God, might dwell there.*

Praise be to the Lord, to God our Savior, who daily bears our burdens. Our God is a God who saves; from the Sovereign LORD comes escape from death."

Raiding Satan's realm was the plan all along. Jesus knew exactly what He was doing, where He was doing it, and to whom He was doing it. Jesus was a big-picture guy. He thought globally, well beyond local communities. Intentionality was the key. He had a determined will. He knew why He was there.

Even in the waning moments of the first century the apostle John, like Jesus, never faltered from the mission. He was a captive set free who took up the mantel and carried on the insurrection against Satan and death: *"We have seen and testify that the Father has sent the Son to be the Savior of the world"* (1 John 4:14). Jesus was sent by the Father to defeat Satan on his own turf and provide an escape from death forever.

I was grabbed from the house of Beelzebul by one of Jesus' committed warriors undercover as a mild-mannered high school art teacher. He risked his job in the public school, his reputation among his peers, and the comfortable confines of staying silent. This brave soldier saw a youth in need of rescuing, and while Satan was bound, he stealthy crept in and snatched another possession away from the Evil One. How do you repay Jesus? How do you repay this teacher for his bravery? You cannot! Just obey, join the insurrection, and go do likewise. In this sense, there is honor among us thieves.

PRINCIPLES FROM THE PASSAGE

- The supernatural world is clearly not bifurcated. It does not war against itself. If it did, it is clear from Jesus' statement, it would fall as a kingdom. Jesus could not be driving out demons by demonic or satanic power. Despite what some might think, Satan and his kingdom are very organized, focused, and tactical.
- Jesus must be operating under the power and influence of the Holy Spirit.
- Part of the Good News includes Jesus as a pillaging invader stealing back from the house of the strong man.
- Jesus invaded Satan's realm. Jesus tactically steals away Satan's possessions (lost people).
- As disciples of Jesus, we are to carry on the mission. We too are to be pillagers of Satan's house. Jesus has bound him, and as Kingdom

soldiers we are to plunder as much as possible, making the most of every opportunity.

- Every exorcism Jesus performed, stole people out of the house of Beelzebul and recruited them into the Kingdom of freedom and life. Each deliverance was another battle that defeated death.

> *Satan has been defeated through Jesus' birth, life, death, resurrection, ascension, and rule. This is one tough Lamb. True, Satan is an awesome foe for us, but not for Jesus. In Jesus, we have victory over Satan. There is no need to fear death.*

DISCUSSION QUESTIONS

1. Several people in this story misunderstand who Jesus is. To believe Jesus is Beelzebul is extremely outlandish. How can you discern whether the misunderstanding is unintentional or intentional?

2. Are you surprised Jesus is portraying Himself as a burglar or robber in this story? Explain. Is that a new picture of God for you?

3. If divided kingdoms cannot stand, how important is unity in the Body of Christ? In your church? In your family?

4. Jesus is the One who ties up the strong man. It is by His authority. It is by His power. How are you doing in helping Him to steal Satan's possessions (lost people)?

5. Do you believe Jesus has really won this war? The fruit of Satan, directly or indirectly, leads to death: ignorance, human systems, illness, natural systems, supernatural systems, and sin. Explain.

6. How do you prepare for battle daily? How do you get stronger? What is your spiritual exercise regimen?

Death, Life & Discipleship:

Sin

"For the wages of sin is death, but the free gift of God is eternal life in Christ Jesus our Lord" (Romans 6:23).

When we think of things that lead to physical or spiritual death, our minds naturally turn to the issue of sin. We've all known someone whose unbiblical lifestyle led to their death. A Google search of the topic will reveal that globally, hundreds of thousands of people died from drug overdose last year alone. Some died by prescribed drugs, and most died by drugs that were not. Poor choices that human beings make kill them. It is a sad fact of a fallen world.

Dysfunctional families and marriages move all too

Sin kills.

often from a wonderful idea to a living nightmare. Most of the victims are females who, rather than being protected, bear the brunt of abuse. This is a sin. It *can* lead to death physically. Sin *does* lead to death spiritually.

Listen carefully. Sin is living in defiance of the way God designed the world. How can I know that design? It is in the Bible. When I purposefully, willfully live in defiance of a known command of God, it is sin. . If I willfully transgress against what I know God has told me, it is a sin. You will sin. At times, you will sin and not be aware you are sinning. Then what? All sin is atoned for by Jesus. All means all. So, you do not have to walk fearful of God's wrath. However, be concerned about your intentional sin. It will kill you. It is death's main supplier. It is the Nestlé of the world of death. Sin holds the number one position in death's market shares.

The Apostle John, after a lifetime of living out Christianity, makes some remarkable statements about willfully sinning. He uses the word *practice* to let the reader know it is a habitual condition of the heart and an intentional choice of the will.

> *"Everyone who practices sin also practices lawlessness; and sin is lawlessness ... the one who practices sin is of the devil; for the devil has sinned from the beginning. The Son of God appeared for this purpose, to destroy the works of the devil. No one who is born of God practices sin, because His seed abides in him; and he cannot sin, because he is born of God"* (1 John 3:4, 8-9).

A follower of Jesus Christ does not *practice* sin. John is drawing a clear distinction between those who live a life that leads to death and those who do not. John also makes it clear in his writings that it is only through a resurrected Savior, living in the follower, through the power of the Holy Spirit, that one can live such a sin-free life. A life that refuses to live in defiance of the way God designed the world. A life that refuses to break God's

> *A life that refuses to break God's heart every day in thought, word, and deed. This is a life lived as a disciple of Jesus Christ.*

heart every day in thought, word, and deed. This is a life lived as a disciple of Jesus Christ.

Now, we return to the continuation of our last chapter, which moves from Jesus being accused of being Beelzebul, to Jesus' warning of an unforgivable sin. Many a person, convicted in heart, has heard this passage and spent sleepless nights wondering, "Have I committed the unforgivable sin?"

> *"'Truly I say to you, all sins shall be forgiven the sons of men, and whatever blasphemies they utter; but whoever blasphemes against the Holy Spirit never has forgiveness, but is guilty of an eternal sin' – because they were saying, 'He has an unclean spirit'"* (Mark 3:28-30).

Back in verse twenty-two, we see that some instigators come from Jerusalem. They have come to end Jesus' ministry and popularity. These were highly educated scribes. They were trained in scholarly study of what we call the Old Testament. They were sticklers for details and knew God's Word thoroughly. They were assassinating Jesus' character by propagating this idea among the crowd: *"He is possessed by Beelzebul,' and 'He casts out demons by the ruler of the demons.'"*

The unforgivable sin is within this context. This helps us define it. Here are elements necessary for one to have committed the unforgivable sin:

- One must be extraordinarily versed in biblical studies, fully informed and fully aware of the nuances of biblical teaching.

- The Greek indicates this is an ongoing promotional idea propagated by the scribes. It is verbal promotion, a public proclamation to win over an audience. It is the scribe's version of a false marketing campaign.

- The source of Jesus' empowerment is under attack. Jesus is being slandered as to how He is empowered. We know He is empowered by the Holy Spirit. The scribes claim the Prince of Darkness gives Jesus His power. This claim is diametrically opposed to sound biblical understanding. They have exchanged the holy for the unholy.

- They are making emphatic statements about Jesus. Those claims of possession do not extend to Jesus' disciples, other believers, traveling preachers, or even this group of curious followers. This blasphemous claim is solely against Jesus.

- The scribes have traveled here, aware of the reports from Galilee. Jesus is doing what no one before Him has ever done. Healing every disease and sickness, teaching the truths of the Kingdom of God with authority, and casting out demons so people are completely restored to mental and physical health. They have heard about it. They have come to see it with their own eyes.

No unholiness exists in the Holy One. Yet, the scribes see Jesus as the incarnation of unholiness. Jesus is pointing out that if this blasphemy *against the Holy Spirit* persists, it will not be forgiven.

A while back, I heard the story of a young man who traveled to Florida during Spring Break. The weather was less than ideal. It was cloudy, rainy, and too cold to enjoy the water. This young man had planned, worked hard, saved his money, and looked forward to a well-earned vacation. He felt like God had let him down and while walking along the beach let God have it verbally. He then wondered if in his self-centered rage, he had committed the unpardonable sin.

Not according to this passage. Had he conducted a long-term campaign to slander Jesus' name and ministry? Was he thoroughly steeped in the scriptures? I confess, he was not. Did he identify what is holy as unholy? No. He was just throwing a spiritual tantrum, as we all have done. Had he seen miracles of healing with his own eyes, and attributed them to Satan? No.

While sin is serious and this passage is foreboding, there is good news here. Jesus makes an amazing proclamation that should resound throughout the world, *"all sins shall be forgiven the sons of men, and whatever blasphemies they utter"* (Mark 3:28). This means it is nearly inconceivable that anyone could meet the criteria of the unforgivable sin, though some probably have. Jesus is ready to forgive all sins. No sin can stand as a barrier to salvation. All sins can be forgiven except one. Millions and billions of sins can be forgiven!

God's grace can be seen in the correction of the scribes. Jesus is even extending grace at this point. Jesus does not issue a condemnation but a warning. The warning is that if they continue down this road, they will end up lost forever. Now, it stands to reason that if a warning is issued, there is still time and a chance to turn around. The point of no return has not yet come, even in this instance. Even face-to-face condemnation of Jesus and an attempt to blow up His ministry to redeem the world, is not a bridge too far. There is always hope with Jesus. Jesus issues a stern correction, not condemnation to an eternal hell. Did they heed the warning?

Sin will kill you. It is the number one killer of all time. Nevertheless, Jesus makes it clear no sin *must* kill you. Think of sin this way. When people are admitted to the hospital for heart issues, diabetes, or bone cancer, the ultimate cause is sin. Similarly, when someone dies from being hit by a car, from a domestic altercation, or from contracting a disease; the cause of death is ultimately sin. The world was changed with one act of disobedience. That one act affected us all. The result is death through a multitude of avenues. If I am killed by a bullet in the Sudan, ultimately the cause of death is sin. If I am beaten, hauled out of my home at night, and murdered by an oppressive regime; the ultimate cause of death is sin. Death is the emissary of Satan— shaped, molded, and mentored by him. Sin begets death.

The big three: the world, the flesh, and the Devil are seeking your destruction. Sin is the way of the world. Sin is the nature of the flesh. The Devil is the author of sin. Where sin lurks, death is just around the corner. Pay attention! Open your eyes! Yet, there is no need to live in fear because we have the One who has overcome the world, the flesh, and the Devil. He lives in us.

PRINCIPLES FROM THE PASSAGE

- Not just from this passage, but from the entirety of Scripture we know sin will kill you.
- Everyone sins.
- The history of humankind is the story of God providing a solution for sin.
- The way of forgiveness has been provided for everyone by grace through faith in Jesus Christ alone. Thus, God has provided a way, and no one need go to hell for their sins.
- Sin is to choose to live in defiance of the way God designed the world. That defiance can be in the way we think, what we say, what we do, or what we do not do. To live in defiance of a direct command of God is sin. To know right and not do it is to be culpable.
- The effects of sin can be seen world-wide, in every human being, at every level of life. The nightly news basically reports on sin. It is all around you day and night. However, you can

85

choose not to commit a willful transgression against a known command of God. We need not break God's heart.

- When we do sin (and we will) God has provided a way out, and we can be forgiven from all our unrighteousness (1 John1:9).

- All unrighteousness is atoned for by Jesus, even the sins you do not realize you commit. That is the grace that is found in Jesus. Jesus paid the price for all sin.

Sin will kill you. Jesus will save you. Through the power of Jesus' sacrificial death sin has been defeated. Those who come by grace through faith have forgiveness of sins. You need not fear death.

DISCUSSION QUESTIONS

1. Have you ever thought you had committed an unpardonable sin? Does it help you to know that every sin will be forgiven, and that committing an unpardonable sin is almost impossible?

2. If the wage of sin is death, can you think of the wages of righteousness, purity, godliness, obedience, faith, and so on? What does that

mean to you? How does it change your daily living?

3. The main three catalysts working on you are the world, the flesh, and the Devil. They want you to sin. Which of these tends to have a greater pull on your life than the others? What can you do to prevent that? What can you ask God to do?

4. Do you have a few close friends who follow Jesus? If not, why not? If so, do you get together and spur one another on toward life in the Spirit and holiness of heart and life? What is the value of this group to you?

5. Sin is the work of the Devil, and Jesus has defeated the Devil. Jesus has provided victory over sin and over the sinful nature within everyone. Can you think of any reason why you *must* sin? Is there any sin you *must* commit? Explain.

Death, Life & Discipleship:

"With" vs. "For"

Spring storms in central Indiana litter the yards with twigs and branches after high winds and even an occasional tornado. Because of this, it was a yearly ritual for my father to tell me "Go pick up sticks." These were words I dreaded to hear, not because it was hard work but because there were so many. It was time-consuming and boring. As a boy, I planned my day of traveling by bike—over bridges and through parks—but picking up sticks was not part of the plan.

In obedience, I would pick up and pile up sticks. I piled stick upon stick and branch upon branch with the glimmer of hope that a bonfire might be in store. One day, it occurred to me that I was not picking up sticks because I wanted to, but I was doing it *for* my dad. It was not a punishment. It was not for reward. I was picking up sticks *for* my dad.

As followers of Christ, we can invest heavily in doing things *for* Jesus because we love Jesus and are thankful for the price He paid on the cross. Even though we know we are not saved by works, following salvation, we can spend a lifetime caring for others, serving others, and investing in others. Typically, this is not to earn our salvation, but we do it *for* Jesus because, after all, we love Him. This is a way of expressing our love.

Do you do things *for* your boss at work? It might be compiling a report, connecting with a client, or beginning a new project. She asks you, and you do it *for* her. However, if you are like most employees, the boss does not do it *with* you. After all, they are paying you and have too much on their plate to babysit you and the jobs they have assigned you to do.

As a stick-picker, it further dawned on me that though I was picking up sticks *for* my dad, what a great experience it would be to gather broken wood *with* my dad. I wondered, as small boys do when they do not like doing what they have been told to do, why my dad did not come and pick up sticks *with* me. I saw a big difference between doing something *for* someone and doing something *with* someone.

The same holds true with discipleship. Discipleship is following Jesus. Being *with* Jesus in ministry and service. Discipleship is not doing things *for* Jesus. It is doing things *with* Jesus. *With* is better than *for*.

My mind began to wander as I traveled the property, numbed by the boredom, which was interrupted by only an occasional sigh. If my dad would come and be in this *with* me, then we could talk, we could have fun, and we could laugh together. Why, we might even pretend we were warriors and throw the long branches like they

> *Discipleship is not doing things for Jesus. It is doing things with Jesus. With is better than for.*

were javelins. There is nothing better than a good laugh with your dad who is doing life *with* you. Ah, but it was not to be.

Jesus made a wonderful "with" statement at the close of His ministry that points us to the crux of what it means to follow Jesus.

"And Jesus came up and spoke to them, saying, 'All authority has been given to Me in

heaven and on earth. Go therefore and make disciples of all the nations, baptizing them in the name of the Father and the Son and the Holy Spirit, teaching them to observe all that I commanded you; and lo, I am with you always, even to the end of the age'" (Matthew 28:18-20).

When making disciples, it is essential to transfer the understanding that the Trinitarian God is with us. He is with us daily. He is with us moment by moment. The author of Hebrews further supports this truth adding, *"for He Himself has said, 'I will never desert you, nor will I forsake you,'"* (Hebrews 13:5). Jesus is always with us. When you undergo hardship, financial collapse, poor health, or family dysfunction, remember you are not going through it *for* Jesus; you are going through it *with* Jesus. The life of a follower is life *with* Jesus, not life doing things *for* Jesus.

On the positive side when you are praying, fasting, studying scripture, worshiping, or serving, you are to do it with Jesus. I guarantee you, from the promises of scripture and the character of an omnipresent God, He is right there with you. Do not go through the motions of doing things, even good things, *for* Jesus. A disciple's life is comprehensively lived *with* Jesus.

The gulf between *for* and *with* is vast and many people have fallen into this chasm under the guise of doing things *for* Jesus. So, what does this have to do with death? *With* defeats death. Attached to the Vine of life, the branch receives everlasting sustenance and does not wither. *Fear* separates the branch from the Vine and it withers and dies. We can have a disconnected heart. When we do anything *for* Jesus, we are separated from Him in the activity, even if our intentions are good. My plan, not His. I do what He wants, not what He has told me. *With* is abiding daily in the presence of the Master. The King of Heaven, who brought the Kingdom of Life with Him, is the One we join *with* in the activities of life. A follower joins Jesus in the journey. Jesus, his Rabbi, gives the directions. The Rabbi makes the decisions. The Rabbi is *with* His disciple twenty-four seven. *With* is better than *for*. *With*, leads to life. *For*, leads to death.

> *"Many will say to Me on that day, 'Lord, Lord, did we not prophesy in Your name, and in Your name cast out demons, and in Your name perform many miracles?' And then I will declare to them, 'I never knew you; DEPART*

FROM ME, YOU WHO PRACTICE LAWLESSNESS'" (Matthew 7:22-23).

If I am with someone, I get to know them. This is a far more conducive way to learn and listen, share, and grow. However, in this passage, the collective voices of those at the Judgment Seat project their disconnection. They were doing all kinds of amazing things *for* Jesus but never *with* Jesus. Jesus' name is wonderfully powerful. Much can be done in His name. Much authority comes from His name. History is full of people and organizations who started out *with* Jesus, then moved to *for* Jesus, and ended up *without* Jesus. The world, the flesh, and the Devil slowly hammered at the foundation of *with* Jesus until a beautiful salvific ministry of service to others toppled under the termites of *for* and the erosion caused by the secular.

Picking up sticks *with* my father would have been much better and much less boring. The opportunity was lost. It is impossible now to return and correct those types of events in our lives. Fear not! We have a Savior. We, who surrender to our Lord, have One who is closer than a mother, brother, father, or sister. I can believe in Jesus and still not know Him. If I have not done so before, I can begin to live life *with*

Jesus today. Today is the day for *with*. Today is the day to begin your walk with the Rabbi perpetually. Today is the day to do amazing things, not *for* Jesus, but *with* Him. *For*, does not work. By living life *with* Jesus, it is highly possible that you might even find yourself less busy, but you will be far more effective.

To be honest, even some of the twigs you encounter may be too heavy for you to carry. The good news is Jesus will not be watching out the window with a face of disapproval. Jesus is right beside you reaching down with powerful hands to lift the load off the child He loves. He will drag it to the dump pile where it can be burned, never to weigh you down again.

Matthew uses an interesting structure in his Gospel as he tells the story of Jesus. At the beginning of Matthew an angel of the Lord reveals to Joseph, quoting Isaiah 7:14, the name of this child born of a virgin. *"THEY SHALL CALL HIS NAME IMMANUEL,' which translated means, 'GOD WITH US'"* (Matthew 1:23). Then, at the end of Matthew we again read the final words, *"I am with you always, even to the end of the age"* (Matthew 28:20). This rhetorical structure is called inclusio and is a tool used by an author to bookend a major theme they are trying to convey to the reader. The theme of God being *with us* is a major point of this Gospel. The Gospel of Matthew was prized among the early church as a tool to train up steadfast disciples.[10] The significance to the fledgling Church under persecution was: you are never alone regardless of your circumstance. I am *with* you. I am doing a great work in you as we walk together. Go tell others that I can be *with* them as well.

The King of Kings came and walked among us. He rose in the morning. He had breakfast. He journeyed from place to place in the region of Galilee. The disciples were with Him. He was with them. He transferred to them all they needed to know, observe, ponder, and understand about who He was and what He came to do. He was God in the flesh. God *with* us.

> *We need never do anything for Jesus because, as our birthright, Jesus is always with us.*

This same King of Kings ascended to Heaven after His resurrection and after being with the disciples as their risen Lord. He now sits at the right hand of the Father and intercedes on behalf of His followers. Nevertheless, as awesome as that is, there is more! He comes to dwell in the hearts of every disciple, fulfilling His promise to be *with* us always even to the

---

[10] Ben Witherington III, *The Gospel of Matthew*, (Franklin, TN: Seedbed Publishing, 2018), 1.

end of the age. We need never do anything *for* Jesus because, as our birthright, Jesus is always *with* us.

PRINCIPLES FROM THE PASSAGE

- We are given a direct commandment from Jesus to go and make disciples. Living in defiance of a direct command of Jesus is sin. If I choose not to make disciples, I am willfully sinning against God. If I make excuses as to why I cannot make disciples such as, "I don't know how," "I don't know enough," "Jesus hasn't told me to make disciples," or "I don't have anyone to disciple," then I am choosing to willfully seek ways not to obey Jesus' direct commandment to make disciples. Ouch!

- The follower of Christ is never alone. Never. God is always with him/her regardless of the situation.

- We are to live under God's command and directives. Our heart condition is never to do things *for* Jesus; we are to always do things *with* Jesus.

- Life lived *with* Jesus is discipleship. A life lived *for* Jesus is never discipleship. This kind of life leads to condemnation and reveals a heart that does not desire to know Jesus. If you do not wish to know or be known by Jesus you will get your wish.

- The very name of Immanuel conveys God's desire to be *with* His people. It conveys the truth of an ever-present Savior who is active in their lives.

When we partner with Jesus in missions to a lost world we do not burn out. When we do things for Jesus, even good things, expect burn out, depression, and a loss of joy. Your insistence to be in control is deadly. Death is defeated when we walk with Jesus. We need not fear death.

DISCUSSION QUESTIONS

1. Have you ever had a job where the boss was *with* you in helping accomplish a task? Share. What difference did it make?

2. Are you a *with* or a *for* person? Explain. If you are a *for* person, what would it take for you to become a *with* person? What change would you need to make?

3. Are you currently obeying Jesus' command to go make disciples? If not, why not? If you are, encourage others to step out and follow Jesus' model. What is the name of the person you will encourage?

4. In what ways is *with* necessary to *know* someone? How does this relate to being a follower of Jesus and making disciples?

5. The punishment for those who Christ did not *know* was for them to depart from Him. He claimed that they practiced lawlessness. What did Jesus mean?

Death, Life & Discipleship:

The Goal of Discipleship

Taking a break one day, I sat by an enormous window overlooking open farmland. Many areas were experiencing power outages. The winds were violently strong, and I was on edge as I looked out and up toward the rain-filled clouds. I was not there long when a turkey buzzard, which is a large scavenger, flew by my window startling me a little. Feeling exposed, I thought it was debris and stepped back a bit. The wind came in surges, and as it did, the turkey buzzard highjacked each swell. The bird ascended and descended. It then ascended again and would remain almost motionless at towering heights. It seemed unconcerned. It seemed to be in a state of peaceful enjoyment in the middle of the storm exposed to the elements.

Over a period of twenty-minutes, the bird moved from stillness to speed to stillness to soaring. Covering amazing distances in a short time, it was being carried along by the wind. It did not fight it. It surrendered to the power of the gales. Doing what it was meant to do, it flew effortlessly, never beating a wing.

The Old Testament term *ruach* can mean spirit, wind, or breath. We know this third person of the Trinity as the Holy Spirit. He is our power source. He is the One beneath our wings who carries us, if we let Him.

It is important to know the goal and destination of discipleship. Where am I going? Where am I leading others? These are important questions, but even better questions to ask are, "Where is the Spirit taking me?" and "Where is the Spirit leading me to take my disciples?"

The rest of this chapter will focus on five interwoven destinations of biblical discipleship. You are sure to flap your wings from time to time—head into a crosswind rather than let it carry you—but God knows that. He is calling you to allow Him to carry you, while you partner with Him in soaring with your disciples to the following destinations.[11]

Christlike love of God. This goal, as well as and the next is clearly expressed by Jesus in this passage explaining the *Great Commandment.* It goes like this,

> *"But when the Pharisees heard that Jesus had silenced the Sadducees, they gathered themselves together. One of them, a lawyer, asked Him a question, testing Him, 'Teacher, which is the great commandment in the Law?' And He said to him, 'YOU SHALL LOVE THE LORD YOUR GOD WITH ALL YOUR HEART, AND WITH ALL YOUR SOUL, AND WITH ALL YOUR MIND.' This is the great and foremost commandment* (Matthew 22:34-38).

Where does the Spirit want to take us? He wants to carry us straight to the Father. Fallen, frail, self-centered, sinful human beings need to be carried. It is impossible to love God on our own. Yet, the commandment calls us to a seemingly impossible heart condition. Fear not! The Holy Spirit resides in each believer. Because this is a reality, the Great

---

[11] Alan Coppedge, William Ury, *In His Image* (Franklin, TN: Providence House Publishing, 2000), 126-134.

Command is possible. Will you surrender to God and allow His love to fill you? Will you allow the Spirit to govern your heart?

All is an exhaustive word. It leaves out nothing. You, and your disciples, as you guide them, are to love God with everything. This is a sacrificial love that costs you everything. This is a love which holds nothing back from the Father and His will for your life. Discipleship training is to take an eternally lost, fallen, enemy of God, and in partnership with the Holy Spirit, bring him or her to a point of complete and total love for God, His will, His plans, His purposes. It is quite a challenge you have ahead of you, isn't it?

Christlike love of others. Loving a loving God is hard, and He is perfectly loveable. However, the second half of the whole command may seem even more impossible to you.

"This is the great and foremost commandment. The second is like it, YOU SHALL LOVE YOUR NEIGHBOR AS YOURSELF" (Matthew 22:38-39).

Love God with all and love your neighbor as yourself. Your neighbor is everyone else besides you.

That includes those who love you and those who do not (Matthew 5:43-48). That includes not only those who view you as insignificant and unimportant, but also includes those who are actively, vehemently opposed to you. In other words, your enemies! Do you model this kind of love before your disciples? Do you not only model it, but do you pray for the Holy Spirit to carry your disciple to this place of divine love? They need your prayers desperately. When they soar effortlessly before their enemies, you will know your prayers have been answered. When those you are investing in selflessly and sacrificially love those who hate them, you will see in them a Christlikeness.

How important are these first two destinations? How important is a Christlike love of God and a Christlike love of one's neighbors? Everything that was revealed by God and written down for us to obey, and every spoken word of the prophets of God, depend on these two destinations (Matthew 22:40). Are you there? Are you leading your disciples there?

The third destination is *Christlike thinking*. Christlike thinking is a transformation of the mind from thinking like the world, and having a secular worldview, to thinking like Jesus, and having a biblical worldview. This is a destination every Christian should not only long for but also strive for.

> *"Therefore I urge you, brethren, by the mercies of God, to present your bodies a living and holy sacrifice, acceptable to God, which is your spiritual service of worship. And do not be conformed to this world, but be transformed by the renewing of your mind, so that you may prove what the will of God is, that which is good and acceptable and perfect"* (Romans 12:1-2).

The mind is the Enemy's battlefield, and rightly so. We grow up hearing untold volumes of wrong, unbiblical, temporal instruction; instruction that leads to death. As we learned in Chapter One, ignorance of biblical truth and Kingdom of God principles can kill you. You and your disciples are to think Christlike thoughts every moment of every day. You will need a zeal for it. It is essential for life, and that is why biblical authors exhort us to saturate ourselves in the Word.

The means of grace such as: Bible study, prayer, fasting, serving, giving, discipling, and worshiping, are the tools for our transformation. God has given us these tools to use in partnership with His Spirit to become more Christlike.

Furthermore, we need to not just know God's instructions. Christlike thinking also involves the will, i.e., the attitude by which we learn and live.

> *"Make my joy complete by being of the same mind, maintaining the same love, united in spirit, intent on one purpose. Do nothing from selfishness or empty conceit, but with humility of mind regard one another as more important than yourselves; do not merely look out for your own personal interests, but also for the interests of others"* (Philippians 2:2-4).

Christlike thinking is a call for all who claim Christ as their Savior and Lord. Christlike thinking is the hard evidence of one's salvation. Is your disciple's mind being renewed? Proverbs 23:7 rings true: "For as he thinks within himself, so he is." Is your thinking Christlike?

Christlike character. We do not have the space here for the volume of references on Christlike character. For instance, think of Jesus' teachings on behavior and character. The Sermon on the Mount is saturated with the standards of behavior exemplified by Kingdom people. The realities of the Kingdom—like being pure in heart; the responsibility of Kingdom people—like being salt and light; the requirements of the Kingdom—like praying, fasting, and even loving your enemies are all found there.[12]

Paul's letters typically start with doctrinal instruction to believers but then typically end with a call to Christlike living. Think of all the "one another" passages. Even beyond the fruit of the Spirit, Paul speaks of courage, persistence, and, of course, godliness. These "one another" passages speak to character and Christian behavior. These traits were modeled perfectly by Christ drawing the interest of those who paid attention.

Our last destination is *Christlike fruit bearing.* Loving, thinking, and behaving like Christ has an impact. Even in this miserable world, which probably loathes everything about you, you can be eternally effective. Jesus tells us that if we are separated from Him, nothing of lasting value will flow from our lives. He also commands us to bear fruit. It is vital that we have hearts filled with love for God and others. When that happens, our lives can produce lasting fruit. Bearing eternal fruit is a sign of salvation and

---

[12] David R. Bauer, *Asbury Bible Commentary* (Grand Rapids, MI: Zondervan, 1992), *834-838.*

sanctification. It is only possible if we are connected to Jesus.

"Every branch in Me that does not bear fruit, He takes away; and every branch that bears fruit, He prunes it so that it may bear more fruit ... Abide in Me, and I in you. As the branch cannot bear fruit of itself unless it abides in the vine, so neither can you unless you abide in Me. I am the vine, you are the branches; he who abides in Me and I in him, he bears much fruit, for apart from Me you can do nothing" (John 15:2,4-5).

Bearing fruit—such as leading folks to Christ, discipling them, and training them to do likewise—is only possible and effective when attached to Jesus. Doing life with Jesus is the life of a disciple. This is the life carried by gales of the Holy Spirit. This is the insurrection. This is the Kingdom of God in operation, overcoming the world, the flesh, and the Devil.

All five of these destinations, for you and your disciples, are only possible by means of the Spirit-empowered life. They are accomplished by walking in step with Jesus each day.

PRINCIPLES FROM THE PASSAGE

- There are many places and destinations to which you and your disciples will travel. These five: Christlike love of God; Christlike love of others; Christlike thinking; Christlike character, and Christlike fruit-bearing are the main destinations.

- All these destinations are biblical and supported by the teachings of Jesus.

- These objectives demonstrate that we cannot save ourselves. They demonstrate we are not essentially good. A radical transformation has got to take place in our lives by supernatural means. Unattached from God we are dead. Attached to God we are alive.

- Life given to us by God is at odds with this world. It looks very different from this world; nonetheless, it multiplies as we engage this world.

- Christlikeness is the goal of biblical discipleship (Rom.8:29).

> *There is no safer place to be than following our Rabbi, Jesus, daily. As He molds us into His image, we need not fear death.*

DISCUSSION QUESTIONS

1. Have you ever known a "Christlike" Christian? Share what made them stand out from others.

2. How does all the Law and the prophets depend upon loving God with all your being and loving others as yourself?

3. In your walk with Jesus, what tool or tools worked best in transforming your mind?

4. Maybe the greatest barrier to the spread of the gospel is that the lives of Christians do not match the words they profess. How can our character match our proclamation? Explain.

5. Are you attached to Jesus? Does His life-giving Spirit flow from Him, as the main Vine, into you, the branch? If not, what step needs to be taken to make this a reality?

6. Would you say your life is bearing lasting fruit? Is it effectively multiplying the Kingdom? If "Yes," where do you see it? If "No," what could change that?

7. Are you taking your disciples toward the five destinations in this chapter? Why or why not?

Death, Life & Discipleship:

Toe Stubbers

Jesus is routinely harsh toward hypocrites during His ministry, just as God is harsh toward hypocrites throughout the Old Testament. Hypocrisy leads to death. Our actions affirm or deny what we profess to believe. In fact, your life choices are crucial! Our choices define the truthfulness of our proclamation. If we say the poor should be fed and do not feed the poor, our words are meaningless. The news on social media, television, or radio is often speckled with these types of reports. A politician took a stand on one thing and then did the opposite. Too commonly, a spouse goes public and breaks the vows they swore to uphold. They confidently do what they promised not to do until death.

More specifically, there are public hot-button topics like climate change, that challenge people to live a certain way to solve a problem. Politicians, media personalities, and entertainers testify to the importance of the cause and espouse acceptable ways to solve the issue. Therein lies the problem. Some activists who claim the earth is in dire straits, live no differently than those who do not. Their carbon footprint is no smaller than anyone else. The casual observer thinks to themselves, "Why should I do what they say? They do not even do it themselves! They say one thing and then do another." Those who do not act on what they say they believe are phonies.

Because of this, Christians must be especially careful to "practice what they preach." Followers of Christ have a unique message unlike any other. It is a pronouncement that has been called the greatest story ever told. Followers of Christ have a monopoly on the combination of two words—*Good* and *news*. There is no other dispatch to a troubled world that can even come close to the Evangelion. This is the message of the Creator God reaching down to save lost humanity—who is without hope apart from His grace. There are no bigger players, themes, thoughts, or truth in all the world. At the center of that good news is an unknown Jewish carpenter, who hails from an isolated truck stop in a land known as Galilee. In fact, His hometown was one of disrepute. People of His day could only wonder, *"Can any good thing come out of Nazareth?"* (John 1:46).

The history of the Church in the world is an amazing story as well. For two-thousand years, the Spirit of God has been moving, acting, and transforming lives, therein giving testimony to His reality and veracity. What started out as a handful of ragamuffin Jews called by a Rabbi, has swept the world. So much so, that a few hundred years ago, some in the Church were asking some crucial questions. The flow went like this, "If we have the greatest message the world has ever heard, bar none; if we have taken this message all over the known world and most of the world has rejected this wonderful message; what is hindering them from receiving Jesus as Lord and Savior?" The term used for this thought is, "the grand stumbling block." John Wesley used this term in his sermon entitled *The General Spread of the Gospel (Sermon 63).*[13]

This idea may have puzzled you a little as well. We know we possess the best message in the world, and that it has been spread all over the world for the past two-thousand years yet, only a third of mankind has believed. What is going on? Has God failed? Is God's Word not powerful enough? After two-thousand years, should not the fruit have been far more abundant? What is this "grand stumbling-block"?

It is quite simple. *You* are the stumbling block. *I* am the one upon which they stub their toe. Just like the secular world and its spokespersons, we are what hinder people from receiving eternal life in Jesus Christ. We are helping people travel down the path on their confused journey to hell. How so? Like Wesley, a multitude of others throughout the ages have lamented, "Christians speak truth but do not live it out." You are most likely among this throng.

---

[13] John Wesley. *Wesley's Works*, Vol. VI. Sermon LXIII, <u>The General Spread of The Gospel.</u> (Peabody, MA: Hendrickson, 1991), 277-288.

We do have the greatest message the world has ever heard. We do have a risen, living Lord who has filled us with His Spirit. Our sins can be forgiven. Friendship with God is a reality. The Good News is being disseminated all over the world. The issue lies in the lack of love in our lives. The issue is the non-transformed minds of believers. The stumbling block is the continued un-Christlike character and our fruitless lives. Why should anyone follow Jesus? To the casual observer, it seems as if Christianity is merely tenets we believe, not a transformed life that we live. Our walk and our talk do not match. We are hypocrites.

> *"If we say that we have fellowship with Him and yet walk in the darkness, we lie and do not practice the truth; … By this we know that we are in Him: the one who says he abides in Him ought himself to walk in the same manner as He walked"* (1 John 1:6; 2:5-6).

Scripture is loaded with these challenges. Are we salt and light? Have we died to self, taken up our cross, and followed? Everywhere we go, do we bring life? Are we lying to

> *Have I ever made a disciple? Is my discipleship method helping others know more about Jesus, or is it helping them become more like Jesus?*

ourselves and to others? Are we walking as Jesus walked? We know what we are supposed to do, and we can call folks to that life, but are we living it ourselves? This stresses the importance of biblical discipleship. It is more than going through a curriculum with others, maybe in a small group or even one on one. As so many have said before, we are educated well beyond our obedience.

Am I lukewarm and has my lukewarmness hindered folks from entering the Kingdom of Heaven through a relationship with Jesus? Have I ever made a disciple? Is my discipleship method helping others know more *about* Jesus, or is it helping them become more *like* Jesus? Do I disciple folks by introducing them to new celebrity Christian authors in an eight-week curriculum, or do I introduce folks to the life-transforming power of the Holy Spirit? Knowing about Jesus is not anything like knowing Jesus.

Christ-like disciples provide an open door to those desiring God. When we disciple toward holiness of heart and life, toward Christlikeness, we remove the grand stumbling block before honest seekers. Living life in the Spirit, living a life surrendered to God daily, brings about a convergence of our walk with our talk. It reveals what real following looks like. Some will be repelled by it. Some will be drawn to it.

A genuine disciple, who possesses the qualities of Jesus and the fruit of the Spirit, attracts attention. Anyone who has defeated death and cultivates life wherever they go is going to draw attention. Not being a hypocrite in this world will draw attention. Genuine, Spirit-controlled believers will draw people to Jesus, the source of their Christlike life. We are only Christlike because we *know* Christ. *"This is eternal life, that they may know You, the only true God, and Jesus Christ whom You have sent"* (John

17:3). To know Jesus, is to know life. To know Jesus is to defeat death. In Jesus, victory over ignorance, human systems, illness, natural systems, the supernatural, Satan, and sin are found. Jesus defeated death on a multitude of fronts before the final knock-out combination of the cross and resurrection.

Those who walk with Jesus and know Him can join the chorus, *"O DEATH, WHERE IS YOUR VICTORY? O DEATH, WHERE IS YOUR STING?"* (1 Corinthians 15:55). We can sing with full hearts, because the last enemy to be defeated is death, and *"HE HAS PUT ALL THINGS IN SUBJECTION UNDER HIS FEET"* (1 Corinthians 15:27). *"Thanks be to God who gives us the victory through our Lord Jesus Christ"* (1 Corinthians 15:57).

I close with this wisdom that Paul gave to Titus. Paul emphasizes a Christlike life. Paul knew the Gospel of Jesus Christ could not advance upon the shoulders of weak, half-baked, comfortable Christianity. Christians could not have one foot in the world and one foot in the Kingdom.

"For the grace of God has appeared, bringing salvation to all men, instructing us to deny ungodliness and worldly desires and to live sensibly, righteously, and godly in the present age, looking for the blessed hope and the appearing of the glory of our great God and Savior, Christ Jesus, who gave Himself for us to redeem us from every lawless deed, and to purify for Himself a people for His own possession, zealous for good deeds. These things speak and exhort and reprove with all authority. Let no one disregard you" (Titus 2:11-15).

Live the life. Walk the talk. Be bold. March in the Spirit. Abide in Jesus. Do nothing that would hinder anyone from entering the Kingdom of God. Be a steppingstone on their journey to Jesus as they observe your life. In doing so, you are defeating death and helping to advance the Kingdom of life.

PRINCIPLES FROM THE PASSAGE

- The most prevalent stumbling block deterring folks from coming to Jesus is the life of most Christians. It does not match what they profess.

- The Bible teaches salvation is by grace through faith. It also exhorts believers to live a radically transformed life that will draw others to Christ.

- When my walk does not match my talk, I can drive people toward hell rather than Jesus.

- Jesus gave us the perfect example of the way to live our lives. My daily life in Christ should look like His.

The grand stumbling block to multiplying the Kingdom is the lives of most Christians. Because their words do not match their actions, it prevents people from coming to Jesus. If you walk with Jesus and walk like Jesus, you need not fear death.

DISCUSSION QUESTIONS

1. Do you come from a region, town, or family in which it is hard for people to believe anything good could come? Explain.

2. When you hear the term "Christlikeness," what do you think it means? What would it look like to *"walk in the same manner as He walked?"* (1 John 2:6)

3. Have you ever been told, or found out later, that your words or actions prevented someone from coming to Jesus? Explain.

4. What is the connection between knowing Jesus and living like Jesus? If you can think of a Christlike person, what makes them noticeable? How did they walk the talk?

5. Why do the New Testament writers continually call people to things like: righteousness, godliness, purity, faith, hope, zeal, and love? What is the connection?

6. What causes Christians to not walk the talk?

Death, Life & Discipleship:

Conclusion

Jesus defeated death on several fronts. He overcame every obstacle. In all honesty, it was easy for Jesus to wield life and smash the works of the world, the flesh, and the Devil. In the final act of God's plan of redemption, however, drops of blood bubbled from His pores. It was at the business end of a cat of nine-tails that His flesh was laid bare. When the nails pierced His hands and feet, blood flowed, and pain electrified His body for excruciating hours. Taking on the sins of the whole world was no simple matter, not even for God. But it was finished! Three days later, after confronting death face-to-face, Jesus rose victoriously as the first born from among the dead. What a glorious day for all of us!

What does this mean for me? Does it mean I am forgiven from my sins? Does it mean that I am justified? Does it mean that I am no longer an enemy of God? Yes, but even more than that, because Christ ascended to Heaven, every believer is indwelt by the Holy Spirit. This makes the rest of the Gospel the best of the Gospel. I can be like Jesus in this world. I do not have to wait until I die! Though I await glorification, Christlikeness is available to me now. Walking as He walked is the call for my life now, not after I die. Today is the day to die to self, to take up my cross, and follow Jesus. Death has been defeated and discipleship lies before me. Will I enter in? Will I ask others to come along? The King of Kings has given me a direct command to go and make disciples. Will I obey or will I freely choose to live in direct defiance of the Great Commandment? The world is waiting. Lost people need me to pick up my sword and join the fight. Go make disciples! Go defeat death on a multitude of fronts.

Make disciples by defeating death on the front of ignorance and a false worldview. God's worldview leads to life—the other worldview and there is only one other—leads to death. In partnership with the Holy Spirit, ingrain, teach, and transform the thinking of your disciples as if their lives depended on it. It does.

Make disciples by overcoming death in human systems. Instruct and live out before your disciples a life that promotes life. This will be a life that brings to light the corruption, callousness, arrogance, and calamity of human systems. Human-centered leadership, institutions, and government refuse to live in the fear of the Lord. The fear of the Lord is to wake up every day and know you will be held accountable for your words and actions; as a result, you live accordingly.

Make disciples by praying for the sick, anointing those who are ill, and bringing the Word of God to the diseased and handicapped. Jesus saves. Jesus heals. Jesus cares. Bring the Kingdom of Life and Light wherever you go.

Make disciples who are fearless over nature, care for the environment, and treasure God's creation. Followers of Jesus should be the most creation-minded folks on earth. After all, you were put in charge of tending the garden. Nature can certainly bring death. Conversely, followers of Jesus come bringing life.

Make disciples who represent Jesus' authority over the supernatural world. Enter the spiritual warfare going on all around you. In Jesus' authority and in Jesus' power, pray against the unseen forces of evil. Pray against the schemes of the ungodly. Act in a Christlike manner toward all. Remember, people are to be loved. You fight against domains and powers, world forces, and spiritual forces of wickedness. Make disciples who are warriors.

Make disciples who Satan cannot stand! Make disciples Satan knows are Jesus' property. The strong man has met his match. Followers of Christ are soldiers of the insurrection—stealing the enemy's territory and his property and disclosing his plans for all to see. Disciples of Jesus do not confront Satan, we let Jesus take care of him while we live peacefully, obediently, and mindfully for His Kingdom.

Jesus saves! Make disciples who carry the good news that Jesus forgives sins and transforms lives. Invest in followers who will not be a stumbling block to others. Be a guide, escorting those you mentor to holiness of heart and life. Make disciples who live life in the Spirit and not life controlled by the sin nature. The world will take notice, and some will want what you have. But remember, you cannot give away what you do not have.

Make disciples who do life *with* Jesus. The world is full of Christians who are doing things *for* Jesus.

Develop intimacy. Develop the oneness Jesus prayed for. *With* is far greater than *for*. Jesus' followers, by definition, are *with* Jesus. That is the biblical view. Watch them carefully, and do not let your disciples settle for anything less than a daily abiding with Jesus. Those kinds of disciples are life-giving, death-defeating believers who change the world.

Making disciples is the greatest privilege in the world. It is heavenly in origin, effective in the earthly realm, powerful when under the headship and direction of Jesus and the empowering Holy Spirit. Making disciples is a charge we must keep. It is a direct command from Jesus to His followers. We have a decision to make. Will we sin and refuse to make disciples? Life and death hang in the balance. Choose life.

When your disciples are ignorant of Jesus' teachings, His commands, and the principles taught in the Word, how will you invest in them and move them from worldly thinking to Kingdom thinking?

In a similar way, where is God telling you to buttress your disciples' understanding of spiritual warfare and the actions they will need to take? "How can I help my disciples move forward?" The previous chapters should help answer that question. This is an insurrection, and the Kingdom needs trained warriors. What about walking in the Spirit? How will they use their gifts? As a disciple-maker, you partner with the Holy Spirit. Where are you taking your disciples?

It is not a discipleship program that will transfer someone from a new believer to Christlikeness. Biblical discipleship, centered on Jesus, transforms the disciple into the image of God through the control and direction of the Holy Spirit. A follower of Christ is God-shaped, not program-shaped. Life is found in Jesus and no other. Continually point your disciples toward Jesus and life. You need not fear death. Jesus defeated death. All other roads besides Jesus, lead to death. I know you believe this is true, but the question is do you live like you believe it is true?

About the author:

Victor S. Collins is Associate Pastor of Discipleship at Kilpatrick Church, where he has served since 2004. He received his B.A. from Vennard Bible College and his M. Div. from Asbury Theological Seminary. He and his wife, Sue, make their home in Lake Odessa, Michigan.

Victor Collins has a passion for Christian discipleship and for individual holiness of heart and life. His desire is to see Christians grow, share their faith, and disciple others. This passion moved him to invest in small group discipleship over the past 36 years. Victor serves as Pastor of Adult Discipleship at Kilpatrick Church. He speaks at conferences, men's retreats, and is the founder of Christian Advance, a website that promotes Christian holiness and discipleship.

Made in the USA
Columbia, SC
29 November 2024

47817212R00072